Staff and Educational Development Association

Lecturing to Large Groups

Brenda Smith

The Nottingham Trent University

SEDA Special No. 1
July 1997

ISBN 0 946815 54 2

Contents

Introduction

Welcome to the Workbook on Lecturing to Large Groups, I hope you will find it useful and informative. You may wish to use the workbook in a variety of ways:

- As an individual member of staff interested in teaching and learning and with a wish to enhance and develop new skills
- As someone new to teaching
- Part of an Induction Programme within your own subject area
- Staff development as part of a course team or programme group

By the end of this workbook you will be able to:

- Select, from a range of techniques, methods to make your sessions more interactive
- Describe the implications of students' Learning Styles
- Communicate high expectations for your students
- Analyse your own presentation skills
- Describe the skills involved in being an effective tutor
- Obtain feedback in a variety of ways
- Enhance your skills of reflection

This workbook has been designed to help you develop new skills and reflect on your current practice. As our time with students becomes more precious it is vital that we utilise it to maximise learning, enhance interactivity and ensure learning is fun. The workbook gives some hints and tips to enhance student learning and to enable your sessions to be more interactive by helping you select from a range of techniques. It emphasises the value of giving and receiving feedback by involving the students as partners in the feedback process.

Most teaching in Higher Education takes place in large lectures, yet this is not necessarily the most effective method of student learning. Lecturing to large groups can be effective for some aspects of learning, while the seminar is more effective for others. This workbook will help you to use the time with large groups to maximum effect. One section is devoted specifically to presentation skills, which may need honing when lecturing to large numbers of students. Teaching Quality assessors/reviewers look carefully at what happens in large groups, so make the most of your learning environment by checking that students can see and hear and that any visual aids can be clearly seen.

Students can quickly become bored in lectures especially if you read your lecture notes aloud, fail to make eye contact, speak in a monotone tone, are disorganised and fail to make the lecture interesting or interactive. Self audit/reflection and student feedback can give you valuable information on your own teaching.

Ensure the students can see where your module fits in to the whole course/programme. Help students to gain a sense of perspective by linking what you are doing now with what you did in the previous lecture and what you intend to do in the next one. The following pages are designed to help you provide lively, stimulating and interactive lectures that enhance student learning.

I wish you every success.

Chapter 1: Getting to Know Learners' Needs and Creating a Secure Environment

When faced with a new group of students for the first time it is very easy to make assumptions about their level of knowledge and understanding. You can go to your first lecture, full of enthusiasm knowing exactly what you want to teach over the next 10 weeks. Time is precious and you have to cover a lot of material in your module. You walk into the first lecture and are faced with 200 or more pairs of eyes, and off you go for the next 60 minutes, hardly pausing for breath.

Finding out Where Students are Starting From

Yet, could you pause awhile and reflect. What does it feel like, sitting out there as a student watching you, pens paused at the ready? Put yourself in the student position. You may be a new student, this could be your first experience of a large lecture. What would you want to know? The following could be a list of possible questions:

- How many weeks do we have you for?
- How is the course assessed?
- What happens if we fail?
- What is your background and experience?
- Will you give us a reading list?
- Will you lecture us every Wednesday?
- How long have you taught at the University?
- Are you going to use a computer projector?
- Do you expect us to ask questions?
- Will we have to participate in any activities?
- Will you give us handouts?
- What will you do each week?
- What happens if we do not understand something?
- Are you going to show videos?
- What do we do if we have covered this material elsewhere?
- What are your expectations of us as students?
- Where does your material fit in with the rest of the course/programme?
- Do we have you in year two?
- Do we get an opportunity to give you feedback on your lecturing?
- Do we have you for seminar and tutorial work?
- How many of your students passed this module last year?
- Do you expect us to copy down diagrams?
- If we fail your module will we be able to proceed to year two?

Why not explore students' expectations and tell them what yours are. A technique you can use here is to ask students in groups to write down all the questions they would like answers to. Record these on acetate and answer appropriately. You do not have to answer all the questions in the first week, but at least you can find out what the key issues are for them. The time spent in this first lecture setting the scene, finding out what students really want to know, and what their starting point is, can be time very well spent.

Think back to some of your best lecturers. How did they set the scene; did they explain clearly about the material they were going to cover and why? Did they give you an overview of what they would be teaching and how this might fit in with your other work - i.e. did they give you the big picture? Did they ask for your comments on the level of difficulty, and did they give you an opportunity to participate and ask questions?

What sort of lecturer do you want to be; approachable, enthusiastic, interactive, challenging, organised and knowledgeable in your subject area?

Do you value students' prior knowledge? Students come from very different backgrounds, different age groups and have different prior experiences in the subject areas we teach. Do you take this diversity into account or do you hark back to the 'good old days' when our students came with a standard set of qualifications, they knew how to write essays and, yes, they could even add up!? Or, do you value diversity and find out where students are, enabling you to take into account the total experiences within the group and start with what they know and then build on this variety of experiences?

Do you ensure that you use language appropriately, i.e. gender-free and not culturally biased? Do we look at the body language and check out understanding or boredom? It may be helpful here to refer to **Chapter 5** on obtaining feedback to check out how you are doing.

Learning Styles

A colleague said to me recently:

> *"I don't believe in using visual aids - I just stand up and deliver my lecture and if the students don't understand it's not my fault."*

I am sure you will have your own thoughts on the above comment, but one thing is for sure - that lecturer had not accounted for the different learning styles of students.

We all learn in different ways, just as our students do, and we need to accommodate these different learning styles into our lectures. There are a number of learning styles inventories around, one of the most well-known being Honey and Mumford (1986). The Honey and Mumford inventory consists of 80 questions, where after analysis a person illustrates a preference in one or more of the following four styles:

Activist

Reflector

Theorist

Pragmatist

When you know your preferred learning style you can select activities that suit you and develop any part of the style which is currently underdeveloped.

The following table (Lewis, 1994), gives a quick indication of your preferred style. Tick column 1 if you agree with the statement and column 2 if you disagree. Try not to spend too long over it, but put down your first thoughts. Leave the column *'Implications for support'* until a little later.

Statement	*Agree*	*Disagree*	*Implications for support*
1. I see problems as opportunities			
2. I prefer to learn from 'real' situations			
3. I see problems as challenges			
4. I like to have time to reflect on what I have learned			
5. I like to listen to what others say and consider all the alternatives			
6. I prefer to learn by watching others			
7. I like to learn things thoroughly before trying them out in practice			
8. I prefer to learn by thinking things out first			
9. I like clear guidelines to work to			
10. I prefer to learn by trying things out and experimenting			
11. I learn best by being left alone to get on with things in my own way			
12. I dislike being given advice until I ask for it			

You can now analyse your results in the following way:

Ticks in **1-3 indicate** a tendency towards the **activist** style.
Ticks in **4-6 indicate** a tendency towards the **reflective** style.
Ticks in **7-9 indicate** a tendency towards the **theorist** style.
Ticks in **10-12 indicate** a tendency towards the **pragmatic** style.

Implications of Learning Style

Activist

If you scored highly in the activist column you tend to be an open-minded and enthusiastic learner. You enjoy new challenges and experience. You like engaging in a range of activities and being the centre of attention within a group.

You are likely to learn most effectively in situations which involve group work, discussion and workshops.

You learn least effectively from lectures and reading and writing by yourself.

Pragmatist

If you scored highly here you tend to be down to earth and practical. You enjoy practical techniques which are relevant to your subject, seeing how theory relates to practice, and you also welcome clear guidelines to work to.

You are likely to learn most effectively through work-based projects and practical problem solving activities.

You learn least effectively from theoretical discussions.

Reflector

You are the sort of person who enjoys collecting data. You will consider all perspectives and prefer to take a back seat in discussions. You learn from listening, observing, mulling over implications and enjoy working independently.

You learn most effectively through project work, lectures and independent study.

You learn least effectively from spontaneous activities with no time for careful plans.

Theorist

You are the sort of person who likes to collect and organise information and deal with models and theories. You love exploring connections between ideas, issues and concepts and are very comfortable with objective facts.

You learn most effectively through problem solving, discussion and questioning theory or reading and evaluating books.

You learn least effectively from open-ended questions, explorative project work, skills training etc.

Your scores may indicate a preference for one or more types. There are no right or wrong answers, for it is your preferred learning style. The categories are not watertight, they do overlap and they can also change over time.

The purpose of the exercise is really to help you think about the learning styles of yourself and those of your students. Our learning styles as tutors do have implications for how we will react to our learners. For example, an activist tutor may be impatient with a reflective student, who might seem to take a back seat in discussion.

What other implications do you think your learning styles might have? Explore your ideas with a colleague, or a team of colleagues.

As a result of your discussions write down one thing you might do differently.

Refer back to the table given earlier in this section and complete the column *"Implications for Support"*

To explore your learning styles more fully, refer to Honey and Mumford, (1986).

Chapter 2: Actively Involving the Learners

When we are actively involved in our own learning we become more effective learners.

We retain:
10% of what we read
20% of what we hear
30% of what we see
50% of what we hear and see
70% of what we say
90% of what we say and do

As Lee Anderson (1996) puts it:

"To teach is to learn twice, to experience a double delight".

Did you know that the average attention span is about ten minutes and that the average length of a lecture is 60 minutes? Yet the evidence is that many staff will lecture for 60 minutes. Student's attention is high at the beginning of a lecture and unless they become actively involved will slowly decrease. To involve students in their learning in an active way helps to bring the attention span back to a peak and thus enhance learning.

Level of Performance

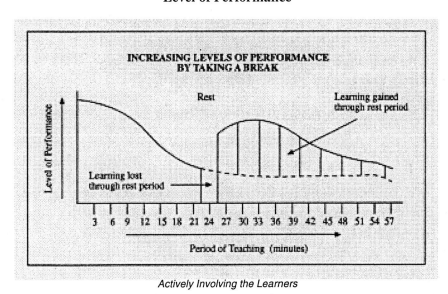

Actively Involving the Learners

There are a number of ways of making your lectures interactive, but the most important issue is to explain to students why you are involving them. To suddenly introduce new and different methods can throw students. From the very first lecture set the scene. Tell the students about your expectations and ask the students about theirs. Try involving the students in their first lecture with you. Treat the suggestions below as a menu from which to select. Try a number of them and evaluate as you go along. Do not expect perfection the first time, you will need practice as well as your students.

Cone of Learning

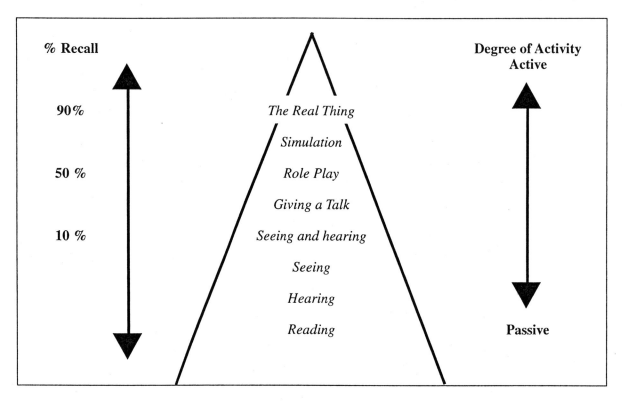

This is a version of the learning pyramid originally devised I believe by Tim Brighouse.

As you see from the diagram above, varying levels of activity can aid recall. Think back to something you have learned recently, such as a new skill or hobby.

What helped you to learn? Write down a few words explaining how you became good at it.....

Race (1993), posed the following two questions to a group of students:

Q. 1 Think of something you are good at - something you know you do well.

Q. 2 Write down a few words explaining how you became good at it.

The answers included the following.....

driving	*lessons, test, practice*
playing the piano	*practice, lessons*
essays	*practice*
painting	*taught techniques, then practice and experimentation*
drawing	*practice, looking at mistakes, not being afraid to make mistakes, experimenting, analysing mistakes*
talking	*practice, discussions with other people*

I suspect that just listening to someone else was not the sole way that you learned either. In the same way your students benefit from active methods and being given practice. Notice also one of the students said "not being afraid to make mistakes". Do you provide that secure environment where making mistakes is seen as a learning experience?

The activities below are designed to encourage you to try a number of different activities that involve the students.

A Round

This is where everyone is given a chance to speak in turn and is a useful way of setting the scene that your lectures will be active. In a very large lecture this may be difficult, but by dividing the students into smaller groups it can be very successful. For example in one of your lectures you could ask students to:

• share with others in their group what they hope to gain from your set of lectures
• talk about their expectations
• mention one aspect that they found easy to understand in the last lecture
• mention one aspect that they found difficult
• express one concern about the course

Each of the groups in turn could then feed back - you could display the outcomes on an acetate for the whole group to see. If the group is really large only take the outcomes from a few groups. Not only does this activity involve the students, but it can give you some really important information.

What questions could you ask in a forthcoming lecture using 'A Round' as a technique?

Buzz Groups

This is where groups of two or more people are encouraged to talk on an issue. It is a useful technique when you are trying to channel their enthusiasm for talking in a direction that you wish the conversation to go. The "buzz" normally lasts for a short time only. Two or three groups can then join together to form *a pyramid*. Combining with another pair or group allows ideas to be developed further. Develop a signal that "time's up" and they willingly return to paying attention to the lecture. During these conversations you could ask them to come up with:

- three questions they would like to ask
- talk about an appropriate article/book they have read
- summarise in two sentences the content of your lecture
- jointly answer ten questions - display the answers on an acetate and get them to read out their group mark

Brainstorming

This is a very useful way of generating ideas and developing creative thinking. The ground rules are that all answers are acceptable and no comments are given in the early stages until all ideas have been given. I believe this technique was first used in the commercial world to generate names for new products like shampoos or hand cream. After producing as many ideas as possible in a few minutes, the group can start prioritising and clustering them. Groups could then vote on their top five favourite ideas - this can also develop the skills of negotiation!

To give students practice, display a paper clip on the overhead projector and ask the students to brainstorm as many creative ways of using a paper clip as possible. Groups can produce 30 - 40 possibilities in a very short space of time. Now follow on with brainstorming possible solutions to a relevant issue from your subject area.

Brainstorming activity:

```
┌─────────────────────────────────────────────────────────────────┐
│                                                                   │
│                                                                   │
│                                                                   │
│                                                                   │
│                                                                   │
│                                                                   │
│                                                                   │
│                                                                   │
│                                                                   │
└─────────────────────────────────────────────────────────────────┘
```

Using Video

Do not feel you have to show 20 minutes of the video. Some of the most impressive inputs I have seen have only been 5 - 10 minutes long. An explanation of why you are using the video and giving out a set of questions before the showing can focus attention and aid learning.

A video can enable you to bring a commercial application into the lecture theatre that otherwise students may not experience. This could range from:

- applications of information technology in a supermarket
- injection moulding
- an annual general meeting
- a keynote lecture

Allowing students 4-5 minutes to discuss the video in small groups after showing can help to clarify issues and lead to a more focused feedback session.

Videos can be recorded off-air, bought commercially or specially produced. See O'Hagan (1997) for more on using video.

Write down one or two videos that you could show over the coming months:

1.	
2.	

Case Study Material

This can provide an opportunity for you to produce real life situations and ask for the students to discuss them in their small groups. It takes far too much time to allow each group to report back in turn, but one comment from 3 - 4 groups can be very effective, especially when the groups do not know when you are going to call on them! Some subject areas have built up a wealth of case study material. If you do not have any try writing some - if based on real work or life situations students are more likely to value them.

Try producing a set with your course team it can be highly creative. For example:

CASE STUDY

Context

Simon was appointed as a new lecturer, having recently come to the University after five years in industry. Pleasant and friendly he gave a good selection interview and although he had no previous experience of lecturing was given the post.

Problem:

Although hard-working, Simon showed a lack of commitment to his work which resulted in student complaints. He also seemed unwilling to ask more experienced staff for assistance and his ignorance of departmental organisation and university systems resulted in a great deal of wasted work for others.

Students complained that he took weeks to return their marked work and there seemed a lack of consistency in marking between students taking the same module.

When lecturing he wrote endless diagrams on the board, leaving little time for the students to copy the work down. Gradually student attendance fell.

Question 1 - What do you think went wrong and why?

Question 2 - What suggestions would you make to:

a) Simon	
b) The Department	
c) The University?	

Demonstrations

What form the demonstration takes will depend on your subject area, the facilities you have in the lecture theatre, how many students in the group and whether students at the back of the room have a good view. Having said all of that, demonstrations can aid learning - you may wish to mimic a person, demonstrate a technique or process or play a musical instrument.

Think back to a demonstration you have seen recently. This may have been given by a colleague or seen on the television or on a video.

List the features that you feel made the demonstration a success.

```
┌──────────────────────────────────────────────────────────────────────┐
│                                                                        │
│                                                                        │
│                                                                        │
│                                                                        │
└──────────────────────────────────────────────────────────────────────┘
```

What advice would you give to enhance that particular demonstration?

```
┌──────────────────────────────────────────────────────────────────────┐
│                                                                        │
│                                                                        │
│                                                                        │
│                                                                        │
└──────────────────────────────────────────────────────────────────────┘
```

Role Plays

In a large group this may be best played from the front of the lecture theatre or room. The use of Role Plays can illustrate for example, controversial issues or put across differing points of view. It can often raise more discussion of the issues than could have been achieved by just telling the students. Some students who are reticent to talk in a large group may be more willing to participate if they are playing the role of someone else. By watching other people play out roles, the retention rate of the major issues can be improved. For example a Role Play of the use of pesticides could involve the roles of:

• local farmers
• local environmental group
• parents
• school children or
• local and national newspapers.

Role cards are produced and the person plays out the role according to the instructions on the card. There are commercial role plays available, but again a small group can produce a set that may be more suited to your own teaching situation. Try and think of some situations that would be relevant to your subject area -

the more topical and newsworthy the higher the involvement of the students. You can also bring in experts from outside the university - a good way of involving your professional business colleagues. In a very short space of time a group of new law lecturers produced some very effective role plays. Why not set your students the task as part of an assessed piece of work?

Write a few possible role play topics below:

>

Tests

Short tests given at frequent intervals aid memory retention. However one way of decreasing stress and increasing student learning is to ask the students to complete the tests in groups. Display the questions and later the answers on an acetate and get them to mark the group next to them. For a bit of fun the occasional prize of a chocolate bar or packet of sweets can go a long way!

Story Telling

Everyone likes a good story! These stories can be real or made up but again are a useful way of illustrating a point. If only more academic books were put on tapes I would be far more knowledgeable! Short recorded extracts from the radio or television can introduce variety and increase attention. Asking colleagues to put their point of view on tapes or interviewing different staff can act as a stimulus to debate.

Goldfish Bowl

This is where a discussion or conversation takes place with students or colleagues looking on as if observing fish in a bowl! The inner circle could be briefed to discuss a scenario, and with an exchange mechanism by which students outside the group wanting to make contributions could replace someone in the group. It can be especially interesting if you get people with opposing or different points of view.

Students can observe the discussion and body language which can lead to some very interesting debates. It is often a good idea to use your colleagues, students or visiting lecturers. To aid discussion, students can prepare questions with one of them acting as the *Question Person*. Topical and newsworthy items relevant to your subject area can provide a really good stimulus to debates.

Chapter 3: Being a Good Presenter

When meeting a new group for the first time there is no second chance to make a first impression!

It is important to set the tone by introducing yourself and giving brief details about your background or experience. You can also alert your students to some aspects of the style in which you will conduct your course or programme. An overhead giving such details and from which you elaborate one or two points can be very useful.

Current lecture groups can be up to 400 students. Giving a lecture can be more like a performance. Being able to talk to large groups of people is not something you are born with. People become good speakers through hard work and practice (Race & Smith, 1996).

Conquering Your Fears

Lecturing to large groups of students can be very nerve racking. Remember it is OK to be nervous - most staff are, especially when meeting a group for the first time. Expect sometimes to feel tension and nervous excitement. These feelings can be turned to your advantage.

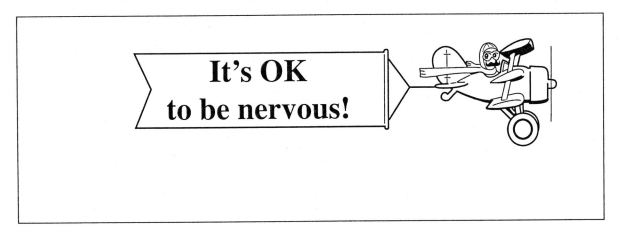

Understanding why facing an audience inspires such fear is the first step to conquering it. Talk to yourself and have the confidence that you will be successful. If you act in a confident manner you will begin to feel that way too. Visualise yourself being totally in control - with practice, confidence becomes natural and comfortable.

Your audience (the students) are not against you, in fact, they want you to do well. If you prepare thoroughly for your lecture, planning the structure, signposting and thinking about approximate times for each section you will feel confident in the quality of your presentation, which will go along way to overcoming your nerves.

> " *The mind is a wonderful thing - it starts working the minute you are born and never stops until you get up and speak in public*" (Roscoe Drummond).

Knowing Your Audience

Don't assume that all the students sitting out there are a homogeneous group of people. Students entering higher education have never been so diverse in age, background and experience. Try getting to know them. Look at **Chapter 1** on **Getting to Know Learners' Needs**.

If possible, arrive before the start of your lecture and chat informally to the early comers. Try and learn a few names each week. Also stay afterwards, you can pick up some very useful information which can make the content of your lectures more relevant. Really think out the expectations of your learners - widely differing ones from yours can be problematic.

Planning and Preparation

It is said that 80% of the success of your presentation is determined beforehand. A well prepared session, carefully thought through, with good signposting, with variety, interactivity and clear learning outcomes is almost a guarantee of success.

Think clearly about what you want to achieve in the session. What do you want your students to be able to do and understand by the end? Write down one sentence that clearly states what the purpose and content will be. You can constantly refer back to this sentence to ensure you stay on track. The overall purpose is best defined as learning outcomes. Make notes on the subject, developing as many points as possible, get all your ideas on paper as key words. Now select three or four main points to be covered and then go through your notes cutting out irrelevancies - be selective. It is better to get across a few points fully than to include too many.

Structure the points you have selected and arrange them in a logical sequence. Most people prefer to work on the body first and then go back to the introduction and conclusion - but you prepare your presentation in the order that works best for you. Remember the basic rule of communication when you are preparing your lecture:

- Tell them what you're going to tell them *(introduction)*
- Tell them *(body)*
- Tell them what you told them *(conclusion)*

There are differences between what can be achieved in a large lecture and what is more appropriate for a smaller seminar group. A seminar should not be used just to lecture to smaller numbers of students! Recent assessors undertaking teaching quality assessment visits stated that many teaching staff did not differentiate between the lecture and seminar.

Consider Bloom's Taxonomy given overleaf (Bloom et al, 1956). Bloom defined a list of hierarchical objectives, starting from the simple and moving to the more complex. Students need to be guided through these stages but the lecture is more successful at achieving levels 1, 2 and 3 and Interactive Seminars, levels 4, 5 and 6. When planning your work refer to the Taxonomy and plan appropriately.

Steps one and two can be achieved through active or passive learning. Steps three to six require active learning which occurs in seminars, laboratory work, but not as easily in lectures *unless you actively involve the students.*

Step 1	Step 2	Step 3	Step 4	Step 5	Step 6
Know	**Understand**	**Apply**	**Analyse**	**Synthesise**	**Evaluate**
define	translate	interpret	distinguish	compose	judge
repeat	describe	apply	analyse	plan	appraise
record	recognise	employ	appraise	propose	evaluate
relate	explain	dramatise	calculate	design	rate
underline	express	practise	compare	formulate	compare
	identify	illustrate	contrast	arrange	revise
	locate	operate	inspect	assemble	assess
		schedule	debate	collect	estimate
		sketch	question	create	
			categorise	organise	
			manage	prepare	

Learning Outcomes

Make sure that the learning outcomes are known to students. Too often, time and care has been taken writing and expressing learning outcomes, which are then filed away in drawers or documents.

Make learning outcomes clear and achievable. Using statements like students should be able to understand the "Second Law of Thermodynamics" is not very helpful. It is better to express such an outcome in term of things students will be able to show for that understanding when they have achieved it (Race & Smith, 1996).

Use language that is accessible to everyone. Do not try and impress your students with jargon that no one can understand. When writing learning outcomes try and use verbs such as: combine, contrast, illustrate, paraphrase, compare, demonstrate, estimate, précis, summarise, categorise, discover, match, predict, change, criticise, design, identify, outline and so on.

Avoid - appreciate, know, understand.

Also group drafting and editing of learning outcomes is always more effective and leads to learning outcomes being understood not only across each course team, but by your students. But do not forget to put your learning outcomes to use. Tell students which outcomes they are working towards in each lecture. Learning outcomes are devised for the benefit of students and need to be able to work well as part of how they find out exactly what they should be trying to achieve.

Having decided on your learning objectives identify the content:

Illustrate your main points with explanations and facts. Give examples that are interesting and relevant to your students.

What supporting evidence can you give?

How will you signpost, help students to see where they are? For example we have just covered **x** and we are now moving on to the second section which will illustrate **y**.

What activities/interaction can you use to aid the attention span and hence learning?

What about audio visual aids? A well executed visual aid can help to focus attention and move 400 pairs of eyes from you to the visual aid! But more about visual aids later.

As you come to the end of your lecture, summarise - highlight your key points again and leave time for questions.

If you are very new to lecturing it can be useful to time how long it will take to deliver each section of the lecture. You may need to leave out some material, or include more to get the timing right, and so it is helpful to write down:

* The essential points
* The important points
* The points you would like to make if there is time

Occasionally when planning you may feel it difficult to break the spell of the blank piece of paper. Try brain storming, teasing out key ideas and putting these ideas on cards. Making a mind map can be really helpful. A mind map is usually done on one side of paper that is placed horizontally.

Tips to make a Mind Map
Main idea - middle of paper
Add a branch from the centre for each key point - use colour
Write a key word/phrase on each branch
Add symbols and illustrations
Use CAPITAL letters
Important ideas larger
Be creative and construct horizontally

Mind maps can be used very effectively when giving an overview of a series of lectures or a programme. If put on an acetate at the beginning and end of each lecture it can help students to consolidate or even refresh key learning points. If you are interested in mind maps refer to Buzan, (1990) and Gelb, (1996).

Openings

The introduction is vital for setting the tone of your presentation, so prepare what you will say and how you will say it. Devise an opening with impact. It should be brief, clear and attract attention. Don't leave surprises or key points to the end of the lecture, grab their attention with important facts and key issues at the beginning of your presentation.

Examples of openings

1. Rhetorical question with an obvious answer, e.g. *"How would you like to impress your fellow students?"*.

2. A startling or surprise statement, e.g. *"The average office worker wastes 4 hours and 39 minutes of work time each week"*.

3. Humour, but with care and only if it is linked to the subject or the students.

4. Reference to a current event or issue, particularly if it is relevant to you and your students.

5. A comparison between industries, companies costs etc.

Openings to avoid

1. Don't repeat the title of the presentation.

2. Don't start with an apology.

3. Don't start say how difficult it was to choose the subject or content, or how difficult they may find it.

Remember, do not start with a negative opening.

And then your conclusion.

Most staff will acknowledge the importance of their introduction. However, few give the same consideration to their conclusion.

"What you say last is often remembered first".

A good conclusion is brief but strong. Try to build up to it, even if you end by summarising your main points. Give your conclusion conviction and make sure it follows on logically from the rest of your presentation.

Types of Conclusion

- Summarise your main ideas
- Look ahead
- Ask a rhetorical question
- Refer back to your opening comments
- Make a direct appeal
- Conclude with a quotation

Using Visual Aids (AVAs)

A good presentation with visual aids is more effective than a good presentation without visual aids. But make sure they are appropriate and complement your presentation. Do not use them for the sake of it, and do not go overboard. It is better to have a few good ones that make your point clearly. An added advantage is that visual aids can help to control your nerves by giving you something physical to do.

Remember research indicates that people retain

10% of what they hear and

50% of what they hear and see

Visual aids can help to clarify and reinforce your message, highlight key information and focus attention. It is still important however to check out exactly what students should learn from each instance of the use of audio visual aids, and also to explain to students why the aid is being used, and what they should do with the information they see and hear. (See SEDA Special No. 4, *Using Varied Media to Improve Communication and Learning,* O'Hagan, 1997).

Quick Tips

- Aids should be clear, easy to read and not contain too much information or elaborate diagrams
- Ensure you are clear about the purpose. Is it an agenda for discussion, a series of questions, an illustration, tasks etc.
- Check you have the appropriate equipment and that it is in working order
- Familiarise yourself with the equipment
- Ensure the students can see it
- Watch out for trailing flexes etc.
- Ensure that any visuals you use can be seen from the back of the lecture room, and that the writing is large enough
- Stand to the side and do not talk to a screen. If using an overhead projector have a paper copy of your slide. This will enable you to walk around the room/lecture theatre and glance down at the material without having to read it from the screen and also enables you to add a few extra notes
- Always talk to your students and not to the screen!
- Keep your diagrams simple - it is better that students understand the work rather than be impressed with fancy diagrams!
- When using acetates use landscape rather than portrait, and favour the upper two thirds of the acetate
- Use a maximum of seven lines per acetate

The most frequent complaints from students about the use of visual aids are:

- Too small a print size
- Not left on long enough for material to be taken down
- Too much text
- Confusing graphics
- Too many acetates

In a large lecture theatre you will need to use a minimum font size of 30 and preferably 36. This also stops you putting too much information on one acetate or slide. Although font size 36 may look big to you, it is not, if read from the back of a large lecture theatre. Walk to the back of your lecture theatre and see if you can read lower font sizes. Don't forget to check with your students that they can see.

Visual Aids 12 Points

Visual Aids 24 Points

Visual Aids 36 Points

Visual Aids 42 Points

When using an overhead projector ensure the surfaces are clean. It is often a good idea to carry round a tissue as the projector easily attracts dust. Familiarise yourself with the machine and work out what all the levers or knobs control.

I have seen quite a few keynote lectures where the overhead projector was out of focus or with a brown fringe and the presenter clearly did not feel comfortable making the correct adjustments.

Computer projectors are easy to use and are becoming more available as the price comes down, but again do feel confident with the equipment. Each room should have details of who to contact if failure occurs or maintenance is required. Try and ensure the appropriate quality assurance arrangements are in place at all times (Brown, Race & Smith, 1997).

Body Language - Creating an Impact

It is not what you say - it is how you say it! Body language can tell you a great deal about a person. Eye contact, posture, gestures, facial expression, voice tone and volume and breathing can all give out messages. (Pease, 1981).

Your students will form an impression of you based on:

Your appearance and mannerisms (**visual**)

The sound of your voice (**vocal**)

What you actually say (**verbal**)

It is interesting and important to realise that the verbal aspects account for only 7% of how we are perceived. How we look forms 55% of the impression, and how we sound 38%.

Your students will know without being told:

- How you feel
- If you don't like them
- When you are lying
- When it is a sales pitch
- When you have given up
- When you are not prepared

Most negative body language is a result of nervousness or lack of preparation. If you are well prepared you will feel more confident and in control, and your students will sense it.

You also need to watch the body language of students, as this can give an indication regarding whether they are understanding the lecture. However it is more useful to make the lecture interactive by asking students questions, to gauge whether they are following the lecture well.

Posture

A sloppy posture suggests a lack of confidence. So stand up straight, balanced on both feet with your shoulders back, without looking unnaturally rigid. Don't stand still - it will make you look more nervous and indeed it is more comfortable to move around from time to time. Not only will this make you more interesting, but you will appear more alert and enthusiastic.

Try not to put your hands in your pocket, or fold your arms rigidly across your chest or fiddle with notes, jewellery etc. - it can all be very distracting.

Eye Contact

Your eyes are a really important feature. Even with large groups ensure you look around the room, but avoid fixing your eyes on any one person. Good strong eye contact that moves around the group will make you appear confident and in control. When lecturing to a large group mentally divide the room into four sections and ensure that you look at all sections. Frequent glances to the ceiling and or floor can indicate nervousness.

Your Voice

The sound of your voice plays an important part in the impression others form of you. Some people naturally develop a good speaking voice, but we can all improve and make our voice more effective. Ensure your voice can project to the back of the room. If students cannot hear they will switch off and then there becomes a tendency for students to talk through boredom, which then distracts other students. If you have difficulty being heard, use a microphone.

Vary Pitch, Tone and Volume

When speaking to a large group you need to add colour and interest to what you are saying. Try taping yourself and play it back. Try to emphasise important words and phrases but don't highlight too many. Use pauses for emphasis and effect. Watch key presenters on the television and listen to the radio. What makes for an interesting voice and what are some of the tips and techniques that newscasters use?

Notes

It is unlikely that you will be able to give a lecture without notes. Avoid writing long and copious notes and then reading them like a script. You are better writing down key words and phrases so that when you glance down you can quickly see where you are, and what comes next. You could use one of the following methods.

Conventional Notes
These could be written notes on A4 paper or card with a highlighter pen to pick out the main points.

Index Cards
Use a card for each main section. Numbering the cards and fastening them together prevents you losing your place, or the order, if they are dropped.

Mind Maps
See the earlier section on Mind Maps. All your notes could be put on one side of A4. The colours help you to see at a glance and your own diagrams and illustrations aid retention.

Handling Questions

Even in a large lecture theatre the use of questions is to be encouraged. Create trust and a positive environment so that students who want to ask or answer a question feel confident about it. Tell the students that you actively welcome questions. You may however wish to say at what times they can ask questions. Questions continually running through a lecture can be distracting for some. So you may wish to say:

> " *I am going to introduce the topic for ten minutes and then I would actively welcome your questions. You may wish to make a note during those ten minutes of what you would like clarification on*".

To encourage questions put students into groups and ask them to come up with at least two questions. This method can especially help those students who may be shy or who find it difficult to speak out in a large group.

You may be worried about being asked a question in case you do not know the answer. If you don't know, ask if anyone else does. If not, say you will go away and look it up and encourage others to do the same. Then make a note to give the answer at the beginning of the next lecture, for you will lose 'street cred' if you ignore it. Never be afraid to say you do not know - that acknowledgement is much better than struggling on and on when you clearly do not know and burying yourself ever deeper in that hole.

So the impression you give is up to you.

Practice and preparation are the key to success - **Good Luck!**.

Finally be enthusiastic about your subject, it is one of the key factors students link to the quality of the lecturers' teaching. Enthusiasm is difficult to quantify - but everyone knows it when they see it!!

Chapter 4: Aiding Student Recall

Helping students to be effective learners is a key task for all tutors in higher education, not only to help them learn a specific subject area, but as part of the skills of lifelong learning.

Creating the Context

It is very easy when you are lecturing to students that all you are concerned about is your subject area or module. Sometime you may fail to 'lift up your head' and see where your work fits in with the rest of the students' experience. This can be a particular issue when you are new to teaching. You will want to get 'your bit' right, you will want the students to like you and you will want to be an effective lecturer.

Having recently been a member of a validating panel for a Masters level programme, this issue was brought home to me quite clearly. Two or three people had been responsible for drawing up the documentation and asking people to write their module specifications. The programme was innovative and well-documented and indicated many hours of hard work. However I felt that some of the staff had put together their module specs without really embracing what the whole programme was like, nor had they shared views or aspirations in any staff development event. The validation Panel felt the whole programme would be enhanced by suggesting that the whole course team spent a day away talking about their part, enabling everyone to obtain a holistic picture of what the year's programme would be like for a group of students.

The question is then, who gives the students the big picture, the holistic experience of the different years of the course programme? Does the course handbook contain details, is it covered at induction, are details available on the Web, or does everyone assume the students will just know?

Students need to have the 'big picture' - a one-page diagram with bridges and ladders (if appropriate) is really helpful. Make it your responsibility to have the full picture. Many of you will teach across different subject areas, but it is very important from the student point of view that you understand the courses/ modules and how they all fit together.

Once the big picture is formed, give your learners a picture of your lectures. A mind-map illustrating your course/module put on an acetate can be really helpful. Displaying this at the beginning and end of every session can help your students to see what you have covered and where you are moving to next.

Think of ways you could help your learners to understand the big picture:

Using Handouts

The quality of handout materials can be a measure of the effectiveness of large group teaching. Quality reviewers look carefully at handouts, to see if they support student learning. The main function of using handouts is to save time, enabling students to listen to what you are saying without having to write everything down, giving them more time to concentrate on the content. Handouts also ensure each student gets the same set of notes and that slow writers, weak language skill students or students with dyslexia are not disadvantaged.

According to Ellington and Race (1993) there are many types of handout used in teaching:

Complete set of notes	These contain the whole of the lecture topic area covered by the tutor and save learners having to write
Skeleton notes	These contain some of the lecture topic covered by the tutor but with blank spaces so that learners have to fill some parts in themselves
Single sheet, short documents	These contain items such as complicated diagrams, sets of data, maps and so on
Help sheets	These provide clarification of more difficult concepts
Bibliography update sheets	These include lists of recently published material
Assessment criteria checklists	These are applied to work learners have already completed and can be self or peer assessed
Printed question and answer sheets	These contain answers to the most important or most frequently asked questions
Miniature flexible learning modules	These contain information, tasks and activities, discussions or responses to tasks

Interactive handouts that involve students in practising and problem-solving are examples of good practice and can encourage active learning. Desktop published handouts can look more credible and professional than hand-written ones.

It is important however to keep these handouts up-to-date. To save large quantities of photocopied material, some sections could be put on the World Wide Web in a *view only capacity*. This means students do not block up the printer facilities running off their copies, but that they are encouraged to read the material and make their own notes. This however can only be achieved for parts of the course. Students appreciate having clear information about the course, dates of assignments, reading lists and so on at the start of the module, with a clear overview of what the module achieves.

Finally, brief students about follow up work. Many lecturers complain that students do not work between lectures, but sometimes that do not really know what they should be doing. Suggest ways of extending their notes, summarising key points, how to structure their reading, where to find examples and which problems to solve. Clear guidelines can really aid student learning.

Give Them a Break!

We all need to refresh our memories and have short breaks - in terms of student learning it pays real dividends.

ATTENTION PROBLEMS IN LECTURES

GIVE THEM A BREAK!

90:20:8 RULE

ADULTS CAN LISTEN WITH UNDERSTANDING FOR 90 MINUTES

AND WITH RETENTION FOR 20 MINUTES

SO TRY AND INVOLVE THEM EVERY 8 MINUTES!

There are a variety of different activities that you can give students to just give them a 'Brain Break'. The five minutes spent on any of these activities can bring the attention back to a high.

Try some of the following:
• Swap notes
• Read a short passage
• Give them a puzzle

The Encyclopaedia Attack

A six-volume encyclopaedia set, which belonged to entomologist Susan Brown, was attacked by a beetle. The beetle's trip began on page 1 of the first book (A-E) and continued through to the last page of the last volume (W-Z).

Being a scientist she wanted to know how far the beetle had travelled. Thickness of total pages in each book 6 cm. Thickness of each cover 0.25 cm.

Question:
What was the length of the journey of our book-biting bug, measured in cm?

Answer _____ (See page 36 for answer).

You can find books of puzzles of this kind in most bookshops. Very few groups come up with the correct answer first time - did you? Think of ways in which you can introduce variety and activity into your lectures. Think back to the lectures you have given over the last few weeks.

List the different activities that you used:

1.	
2.	
3.	
4.	
5.	

Lecture Summaries

I have seen a number of staff go into a lecture with a wad of acetates and then expect the students to copy them down verbatim. There are no extras, no expansion of parts, no discussion and no interaction. What a waste of time - it is passive and can be boring!

Reduced OHP Acetates Handouts

Rather give the students copies of the handouts as miniatures and encourage them to make expansive notes around yours to aid their learning. For example, one piece of A4 paper, copied back to back, can hold a full lecture in miniature form. A good way of saving the forests, but also one page printed back to back is quicker, cheaper to print and to distribute, especially to up to 400 students. The miniatures can be produced very easily using modern presentation software such as Powerpoint in Microsoft Office.

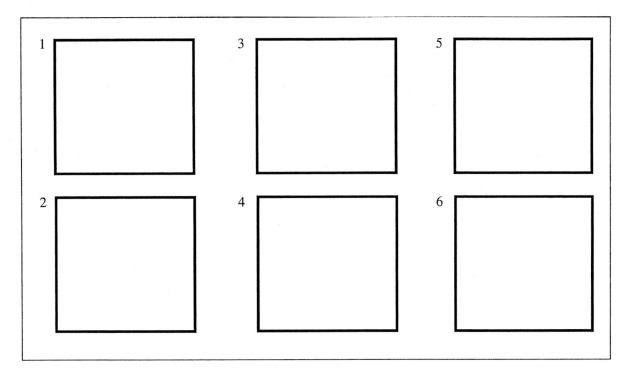

Diagrams unlabelled with gaps for students to complete aid retention and memory, and keep them involved in the learning process. Encourage the students to produce some of their material in diagrams, using whatever mental images come to them. Handout skeletons can also encourage students to attend lectures if they are to obtain a complete picture.

When using graphs, label the axis but let the students do the plotting or omit some critical figure from a table of data, or partially complete a calculation, leaving space for them to work it through.

Note Taking

Do not assume students will be good at taking notes! Some students will expect to take notes in a certain way because that is what happened at school, or with other lectures. Most will take notes in a linear form. You may wish to introduce mind mapping as another way of aiding recall.

Whatever method you use, briefing a class will help. You may say 'You don't need to take notes here, just listen and then I will repeat it and give you an opportunity to take notes'. This helps to ensure proper attention as opposed to getting everything down you say without any understanding.

A good structure to a lecture can help students, especially if you tell them when you are moving to other sections. Encourage students to swap notes with the person sitting next to them. Give them time to read each others' notes, and then give some feedback. For example,

The best thing about your note-taking is........

```
┌─────────────────────────────────────────────────────────────┐
│                                                             │
│                                                             │
│                                                             │
│                                                             │
│                                                             │
│                                                             │
└─────────────────────────────────────────────────────────────┘
```

One suggestion I would like to make to you is........

```
┌─────────────────────────────────────────────────────────────┐
│                                                             │
│                                                             │
│                                                             │
│                                                             │
│                                                             │
│                                                             │
└─────────────────────────────────────────────────────────────┘
```

To encourage students to read through their notes, allow five minutes towards the end of your lecture. Suggest that they mark sections on which they would like further clarification, or ask questions when they do not understand. Having a pack of scrap paper for students to write their questions on, and which they can place in a box at the end of the lecture, can provide useful material for the start of your next session.

At the end of the lecture, ensure that the students are clear about your aims and learning outcomes, and check out with them that they feel you have achieved them.

Memory Techniques

Having a good memory is a really useful skill. Yes, developing your memory is a skill and there are techniques that you can practise and pass on to your students that would make their life easier.

There are so many situations where having a good memory is useful. For example being introduced to new staff and remembering their names, shopping in a supermarket, remembering facts and figures or key issues arising from conversations or departmental meetings. There are a number of books or tapes that you could refer to. See Buzan (1995 (revised), 1988, 1989).

```
┌─────────────────────────────────────────────────────────────┐
│                                                             │
│   ANSWER To the Encyclopaedia Attack (page 33) is 26.5 cm.  │
│   Remember Page 1 of the set                                │
│   A to E, starts on the right hand side when viewing the    │
│   book on the shelf!                                        │
│                                                             │
└─────────────────────────────────────────────────────────────┘
```

Chapter 5: Obtaining and Giving Feedback

Tutor to Students

If your goal is merely to deliver the session, feedback is irrelevant. If however you wish the students to "learn effectively" then feedback is vital.

Firstly, feedback can be from you the tutor to the students on a piece of work or secondly, on students' contribution to a lecture or seminar. Both are very important, but you need to be clear about the purposes of the feedback and to share those purposes with your students. When giving feedback to students always start with something positive, but also ensure that they are told how they may enhance the piece of work. Try not to use final language such as excellent for even the excellent student can be 'stretched' to do even better. Suggest for example that they read a new article.

Students to Tutor

A second type of feedback is from the students to you and this feedback is equally important, but one that is often omitted. You may hold the view that you know you are a good lecturer, and if your students don't learn or attend your lectures, then it is their fault not yours. If you are one of these staff I would ask you to reconsider that point of view.

Receiving feedback from students can put us on the defensive. I remember giving students a very long questionnaire that asked everything from how difficult they found the lectures, what helped them to learn, to how easily could they read my writing on the acetates. Imagine my horror when they all said they could not read my writing. I was tempted to bin the set of responses! Then I reflected, if I had wanted feedback I must be prepared for the consequences and I know I am better at some aspects of teaching than others.

Those comments on my writing did actually encourage me to learn to word process very early on, and now with new computer software packages presentations can be produced very professionally. We need to believe however, that no matter how experienced we are, situations change, students change and therefore a good tutor will continually reflect on what could have been done differently, better, or what our students would like more of. This reflective practice I believe is essential to learning, and although painful at times, is in the long run exceptionally rewarding. Someone once said that when it is painful we can often learn more.

A very quick way of gathering student views on our teaching is to use a technique I learned form Professor Phil Race called the *Stop, Start, Continue* Method. These three words can be put in large letters across an acetate and then ask the students to jot down on a piece of paper or post-it what they would like you to STOP doing, START to do or CONTINUE to do. Then collect them in, or display them around the room (depending on the size of the group).

STOP	START	CONTINUE

This activity can provide you with some really interesting feedback. Our perceptions of how things are going can be very different from those of our students, but can provide us with really useful information.

Another quick way of finding out how you are doing is to ask the following sorts of questions:

- How many of you would like me to give you another example?
- What do you think are the three most important aspects of today's lecture?
- What have you found to be the most difficult aspects of this lecture?
- What have you found easy about this lecture?
- What would you like me to clarify for the next lecture?

You could ask all students to respond or alternatively ask ten different students each week and record their answers on an acetate, displaying it at the beginning of the next session. This then allows you an opportunity to discover what certain students find difficult or easy. The answers from this small group of students can easily be checked out with the full group at the beginning of the next lecture.

The Instant Questionnaire

For this you can devise any number of short questions, which can be read out or displayed on an acetate. The students list the number of questions to be answered down the side of a paper and then list A, B, C, D or E depending on their answer.

> A = Always true for me
> B = Often true for me
> C = Sometimes true for me
> D = Seldom true for me
> E = Never true for me.

For example the questions could be

> 1 I understand the lecture content
> 2 The pace is too slow
> 3 The lecture material is too difficult
> 4 We have covered this material before
> 5 Paying attention is really difficult

All the student then hands in is the number of questions with the appropriate letter of the alphabet by the side:

> 1. B
> 2. C
> 3. A
> 4. D
> 5. E

These answers could be dropped into a box as the students leave the lecture. This method can be a quick way of obtaining feedback.

Another One Minute Questionnaire

The best thing about this session was ....

The worst thing about this session was ....

For me the easiest part of this session was ......

For me the hardest part of this session was ......

The Random Student Method

This is where every few weeks you select six students at random to stay behind and give you feedback. This could be obtained by asking set questions or by listening to their issues. Six students can only give you a snapshot, but because the issues concern them it can provide really useful and relevant information. It also prevents issues building up. Their comments can be dealt with quickly and appropriately and it can foster good staff student relationships. If it is difficult for students to stay beyond a lecture ask the students to complete the questionnaire electronically.

However in all these methods of collecting feedback the students need to feel secure in the knowledge that they will not suffer for giving feedback. Students really welcome staff who are approachable, available and who accept their comments in a supportive and constructive environment. Do not forget to tell the student what you intend to do as a result of their feedback.

Tutor to Tutor

Invite a colleague in.

We have a lot to learn from our colleagues by just watching them in action and talking to them about their expectations and why they used certain techniques. Invite a colleague to one of your future lectures. Meet before the lecture and talk about your aims and learning outcomes. Following on from the lecture ask for feedback from the colleague. What did your colleague feel you did particularly well, and what suggestions are there for enhancement.

Studies by Entwhistle and Tait have focused on students' perceptions of courses, citing five factors that contribute to depth and quality of student learning:

• Good teaching
• Clear goals
• Appropriate workload
• Appropriate assessment
• Emphasis on independence

A number of observation sheets are available and you may wish to contact your Educational or Staff Development Unit to view a selection. A very simple but useful framework might be:

Three things that went really well:

1

2

3

One suggestion for enhancement

As you feel more confident with a colleague additional questions you might wish them to ask you could include:

What do you hope to achieve in this session?

What structure do you have for this session?

How do you hope to involve the students?

What audio visual aids do you intend to use?

How will you encourage students to ask questions?

How will you check on student learning?

What support material will you give out?

How will you conclude the session?

Currently Teaching Quality Assessors in the UK (HEFCE, 1996) use an evaluation form that asks for:

Teaching. What are the particular objectives planned for this session?

Please comment on the effectiveness of each of the following elements and the extent to which the planned objectives are achieved	
Planning	
Content	
Methods	
Pace	
Use of examples	
Overall comments:	

Student participation - to what extent was student participation intended and how far did it occur as planned; what evidence was there of student engagement with the session; what evidence was there of the learning objectives being achieved?

Accommodation and Resources: how effective was the use of the room and layout, specialist equipment and material, visual aids, IT, etc.?

```
```

Overall Quality of the Session: judgement of the appropriateness of the specific session objectives and their achievement to the overall achievement of objectives

Strengths	
Weaknesses	
Other comments:	

The Giving and Receiving of Feedback

Think back over the last, say, ten years and reflect on any feedback that you have received, both positive and negative. This feedback may have been in connection with a piece of work you did, a hobby or new skills you learned.

Was the feedback always as helpful as it could have been, did it aid or hinder learning? Make a few notes in the table below about the most effective forms of feedback and how they were given. What did you learn from the different ways that you were given feedback?

Feedback given on a a new skill, piece of writing or hobby:	Positive aspects:	Negative aspects:	What did you do differently as a result of that feedback?
1			
2			
3			
Lessons learned from receiving feedback:			

Having given a recent presentation to a group of academic staff on a project for which I had received some quite substantial funding, I was met afterwards by one member of staff who told me quite forcibly that this department did not use clip art or borders around their acetates, and had I realised that the colour of the border was the colour of the nearby Shopping Centre! (I think it could be described as going straight for the jugular!).

Notice how some members of staff can give really useful feedback and in a supportive way. I always encourage staff to give feedback using the *Sandwich Method*. Start and end with positive feedback (the two layers of bread) and the filling could be something you might like to think about or something you might do differently. This method not only encourages staff to be confident in their methods, but encourages reflection leading to what might be done better or differently.

Try and create a climate where feedback is positively encouraged and do try and give positive feedback upwards, sideways and down. By that I mean everyone likes positive feedback - don't forget your line manager or senior managers too!

Another way is to receive feedback as a group, where you encourage all members to engage in open and critical debate, where all comments are taken seriously and discussed, but in a supportive and non-threatening environment. We need people to disagree with us, it can lead to healthy discussions and help us to question preconceived values or beliefs.

This sort of environment is especially useful when we come to evaluate our courses or programmes or are planning new programmes. Once a year it is a good idea to stand back and say 'what can we be proud of' and 'what might we do differently or better next year'. Involving students in these discussions can be really productive and helpful and encourage students to realise that you do take feedback seriously and want to listen actively to their comments and engage them as partners in the process.

Being a Reflective Practitioner

Give yourself some feedback!

Write down one aspect of your teaching that you do really well.

```
┌─────────────────────────────────────────────────┐
│                                                 │
│                                                 │
│                                                 │
│                                                 │
│                                                 │
│                                                 │
└─────────────────────────────────────────────────┘
```

Write down one aspect of your teaching that you would like to enhance.

```
┌─────────────────────────────────────────────────┐
│                                                 │
│                                                 │
│                                                 │
│                                                 │
│                                                 │
│                                                 │
└─────────────────────────────────────────────────┘
```

Share both aspects of your teaching with a colleague. Discuss ways in which you can help staff receive both positive and constructive feedback.

GOOD LUCK!

Chapter 6: Student Views: Features of the Ideal Lecturer

If we ask students what are the characteristics of a good lecturer, the detail would vary from student to student and slight differences would occur in different subject groups and in groups from different cultures. However we can draw on the outcomes of a number of these studies to obtain a reasonably generalisable picture.

In drawing on these studies, however, I would like to make it clear that we do not want clones all churning out wonderful acetates and lecturing in the same way, we want staff to maintain their personalities and do things in different ways, otherwise our students will not benefit from the diversity of staff. The purpose in highlighting certain key characteristics is to draw your attention to those aspects of teaching that students welcome as enhancing their learning.

Being a good teacher in a study in the USA (Attitudes and activities of full-time faculty members, 1993) was rated as essential or a very important goal by 97.6% and 95.5% of professors at public and private universities and by 98.3% and 99% of professors at public and private four-year colleges, respectively. Therefore, it is clear that the provision of high-quality instruction is valued not only by students, parents, state legislators, and the general public, but by faculty staff as well.

Research has produced many student-generated lists of the characteristics of the good or ideal teacher (e.g., Feldman, 1988; Goodwin and Stevens, 1993; Runco and Thurston, 1987; Waters et al., 1988). These lists of characteristics vary in specificity.

Waters et al. (1988) found three broad categories of responses when they asked students to write down the qualities of both excellent and poor teachers that most influence their evaluations.

Personal characteristics   described personal attributes of the ideal professor in general.

Interpersonal characteristics   described personal attributes and behaviours of the ideal professor that related to interpersonal relationships with students, and

Class characteristics   described personal attributes and behaviours of the ideal professor that related specifically to the class.

In a study by Smith et al. (1994), respondents were asked to fill out a questionnaire:

Please take a few minutes to think about your ideal college professor (lecturer). This may reflect one person, or may be a combination of the qualities of different professors. Keep this ideal image in your mind as you answer the following questions. Please answer as completely as you can, providing as much detail as possible.

Immediately following these instructions was the question, *"What qualities do you believe the ideal professor (lecturer) should have?"* and *"What communication skills, both verbal and non-verbal, characterise the ideal professor (lecturer)?"*

The Mean Proportion of each category for males and females gave the following response:

Empathic	*Provides and requests feedback*
Good speaker	*Goes beyond lecture*
Approachable	*Organised*
Knowledgeable	*Makes eye contact*
Encourages interaction	*Dedicated to teaching*
Enthusiastic	*Presents a professional appearance*
Moves about the classroom	*Gives interesting assignments*
Uses expressive voice	*Interesting*
Clear and informative	*Manages time effectively*
Humorous	*Engenders respect*
Fair	*Responds to non-verbal behaviour*
Relates to students as equals	

"For the entire sample, the **personal characteristics** of *knowledgeable* and *enthusiastic*, the **interpersonal characteristics** of *empathic* and *approachable*, and the **class-related characteristics** of *good speaker, encourages interaction, moves about the classroom*, and uses *expressive voice* all ranked within the top third of the prototype.

Thus, it is apparent that the three general categories of personal, interpersonal, and class related characteristics are salient and important to undergraduate students." (Smith S W et al. 1994).

I wonder what answers your students would give to the following question:

"What qualities do you believe the ideal lecturer should have?"

When you have your own list, why not ask your students to rate you against it?

Students have indicated some common weaknesses in lecturing:

- Saying too much too quickly
- Assuming too much knowledge
- Forgetting to provide a summary
- Timing
- Not leaving time to copy diagrams

- Not stressing major points
- Not confident about own knowledge
- Not linking sections together
- Not organising sections clearly
- Using too much technical language too quickly

To assess your own teaching quality refer to: ***Assess Your Own Teaching Quality*** (Brown & Race, 1995).

Chapter 7: Manifesto for Learning

I would like to summarise lecturing to large groups by sharing with you my personal manifesto for learning. This consists of ten tips, which I would ask you to score yourself against. You may or may not agree with the statement, or you might like to set yourself an action plan about something you wish to achieve, or do better.

Manifesto for learning	I do this often	I do this sometimes	I don't do it
1 **Help students to learn with the big picture** I give my students a view of the whole module or course, or where appropriate, a view of the three or four year programme			
2 **Value prior knowledge** I value diversity and take this into account in my lectures and when setting assessed pieces of work. I take into account the total experiences within the group and start with what they know and build on that			
3 **Help students to assess and then understand their learning styles** I help my students to analyse and work out their preferred learning style, helping them to extend their styles if appropriate. I take into account different learning styles when lecturing to large groups			
4 **Help students and staff to understand assessment and use it appropriately** I assess my students using a variety of methods to test a range of their skills. I also liaise with my colleagues to ensure a spread of work for students and a spread of submission dates for assignments			
5 **Encourage your students to engage in self and peer assessment** I encourage my students to use both peer and self assessment and actively engage them in formulating the criteria. I also give learners experience of giving and receiving feedback in a secure environment			

6 Value feedback I value feedback from my colleagues and actively encourage them to sit in and observe my lectures			
7 Help students to develop learning skills I ensure that appropriate learning skills are integrated into courses at an appropriate time and level			
8 Encourage interactivity I believe in encouraging students to learn by being motivated, by doing, by being given an opportunity to practice and then be given feedback on the outcome			
9 Encourage learning along the way I encourage students to learn throughout my course and not just at the end. I devise a variety of techniques to encourage this from the setting of short early tasks to answering questions in groups			
10 Make learning fun I believe that students learn better when they are finding the work enjoyable. I actively try to create an atmosphere of security and excitement in the subject area			

You have now come to the end of this workbook on Lecturing to Large Groups. I hope you have found it useful and that it has motivated you to reflect on your teaching and to try some enhancements.

To help you with this the Personal Action Plan on the next page offers some helpful guidelines.

Personal Action Plan

Name: Date:

What specific changes do you want to make?

What will your first steps be?

What processes will you have to go through to achieve this change?

What deadlines will you have to meet?

Whose help or agreement will you need?

Who or what will support you?

Who or what will hinder or constrain you?

How might you overcome these problems?

How will you be able to measure the extent to which you have been successful?

Now identify your next target!

References

Anderson L (1996) *On Becoming a Maker of Teachers: Journey Down a Long Hall of Mirrors in* - Boud D, Cohen R, Walker D (Editors) (Reprinted - 1996) Using Experience for Learning. The Society for Research into Higher Education and Open University Press.

Attitudes and activities of full-time faculty members (1993, August 25). The Chronicle of Higher Education, p35.

Bloom B, Englehart M, Furst E, Hill W & Krathwohl D (1956) *Taxonomy of Educational Objectives.* New York: David McKay.

Brown S, Race P (1995) *Assess Your Own Teaching Quality*. London: Kogan Page.

Brown S, Race P, Smith B (1997) *500 Tips on Quality Enhancement.* London: Kogan Page.

Buzan T (1990) *The Mind Map Book. Radiant Thinking The Major Evolution in Human Thought.* London: BBC Publications.

Buzan T (1995) *Use Your Memory*. London: BBC Publications.

Buzan T (1988) *Harnessing the ParaBrain. How to achieve a significant increase in your mental powers.* Cambridge: Colt Books.

Buzan T (1989) *Use your Head*. London: BBC Publications.

Ellington H & Race P (1993) *Producing Teaching Materials: A Handbook for Teachers and Trainers*. London: Kogan Page.

Feldman K A (1988) *Effective College Teaching from the students' and faculty's view: Matched or mismatched priorities?* Research in Higher Education, 28, 291-344.

Gelb M (1996) *Mind Mapping. How to wake up your brain and liberate your natural genius* (A series of eight audio cassettes). Nightingale Conant. Long Road, Paignton, Devon TQ4 7BB. Tel: 01803-666100 Fax: 01803-557148.

Goodwin L D & Stevens E A (1993) *The influence of gender on university faculty members' perceptions of "good" teaching*. Journal of Higher Education, 64, 166-185.

Higher Education Funding Council for England, *Assessors' Handbook*, October 1996 to September 1998.

Honey P & Mumford A (1986) *Using Your Learning Styles*. Maidenhead, Berkshire: Printique.

Lewis R & Freeman R (1994) *How to Manage Your Study Time*. London: Harper Collins with NEC.

O'Hagan C M (1997) *Using Varied Media To Improve Communication and Learning*. SEDA Special No. 4. Birmingham: SEDA.

Pease A (1981) *Body Language. How to read others' thoughts by your gestures*. London: Sheldon Press.

Race P (1993) *Never Mind the Teaching Feel the Learning*. Birmingham: SEDA.

Race P & Smith B (1996) *500 Tips for Trainers*. London: Kogan Page.

Ramsden P *Learning to Teach in Higher Education*. London: Routledge.

Runco M A & Thurston B J (1987) *Students' ratings of college teaching: A social validation*. Teaching of Psychology, 14, 89-91.

Smith S W, Medendrop C L, Ranck S, Morrison K & Kopfman J (1994) *The prototypical features of the ideal professor from the female and male undergraduate perspective: The role of verbal and non-verbal communication*. Journal on Excellence in College Teaching, 5 (2), 5-22.

Waters M, Kemp E, Pucci A (1988) *High and low faculty evaluations: Descriptions by students*. Teaching of Psychology, 15, 203-204.

The author is Teaching and Learning Quality Manager at the Nottingham Trent University, is responsible for promoting innovation in teaching and learning across the University and is an international consultant and workshop presenter in higher education.

Brenda.Smith@ntu.ac.uk
www.ntu.ac.uk/talec/

to effective participation by those who are not presenting at a given time.

TV Production:

If you are looking for an activity which really develops good teamwork, try a production in a TV Studio. What is produced may be less important than the activity itself, but can add to the interest and excitement. You will need access to a TV studio where students are allowed to be producers - behind the cameras, in the control room etc. Actually there is nothing very complicated about the equipment in a simple studio production, just a few DO's and DON'Ts. Good technical staff will be happy to advise and support your students - and have a bit of fun themselves.

Finding something to produce is not very difficult. For example, think of a TV show you can copy. I have produced Call My Bluff, and Crown Court, with students in front of and behind the cameras. Another production was Booze, looking at various aspects of alcohol consumption, and including a videotaped interview with a pub landlord, finally all put together in a studio production.

I don't think I have done anything which has better brought out the hidden depths and talents of students - as 'Robert Robinson', as a barrister, as a witty panel game member, as a TV producer - or which has yielded such team commitment and responsibility.

Multimedia Production:

Students (as a small group) produce a simple multimedia information programme or tutorial. A simple authoring shell can be used, and students will need to collect or make the necessary variety of audio and visual resources. Students can try 'virtual tours' where a place or venue is explored interactively through hot-linked photographs and graphics, or create tutorials on something they, say, studied in their first year - an incentive might be to actually test it on a student cohort. Some of the productions might actually benefit future students, or give you some ideas for producing such resources yourself.

KEY: Mixed media activities and presentations are a great way of developing teamwork and communication skills - they can also bring to the fore hidden talents in your students.

Chapter 13: Further Help

General:

Books in this area go out of date quite quickly - as this one will! - particularly where technologies are developing rapidly, as in multimedia and the WWW. For a more extensive discussion of the well-established media, a good reference book is:

> Ellington Percival and Race (1993), *Handbook of Educational Technology,* 3rd ed, London: Kogan Page

and a good Web site is:

> Edu-Tech, Educational Technology Information and Resources. A database with a search engine and hot links, including a list of UK University Educational Technology Centres - www.warwick.ac.uk/ETS/edu-tech/index.html

Video:

BUFVC, the British Universities Film and Video Council produces a regular newsletter, Viewfinder, with useful reviews of educational videos as well as articles. Various memberships are available, including an add-on service which enables members to obtain copies of off-air programmes they have missed (eg after watching a programme on TV at home you think, "I could have really used that on my course.")

> BUFVC, 55 Greek Street, London W1V 5LR
> BUFVC@open.ac.uk

SHOTLIST: This is a scheme organised by the Educational Broadcasting Services Trust to create copyright-free educational video for UK higher education. You can buy a master tape, freely edit it, digitise it, give it a different commentary etc. Master tapes are less than £100, and the subject list is expanding.

> EBS Trust, 36-38 Mortimer Street, London W1N 7RB
> Tel: 0171 580 6246

VESOL: To obtain more information about this system described in the chapter Creating and Customising Video try:

> O'Hagan C M (1995), Custom videos for flexible learning, *Innovations in Education and Training International*, 32.2, May 1995, p.131-138

and

> the VESOL Web site: www.derby.ac.uk/cedm/vesol/home.html

Computers:

CTI: Computers in Teaching Initiative. There are 24 subject-based centres offering help on using computers in teaching and learning:

www.cti.ac.uk

TLTP: Teaching and Learning Technology Programme. Details of 78 projects developed in the UK (including VESOL) with hot links to sites. Will expand to include information about dissemination projects funded from February 1988 in TLTP Phase III.

www.tltp.ac.uk/tltp

MAILBASE: electronic discussion lists for higher education. There are over 1000 -something for just about every subject or interest group in research, and teaching and learning:

www.mailbase.ac.uk/

TOTAL: Tutor Only Transfer of Authored Learning. Multimedia shells which enable teachers to put materials into a Multimedia format without the usual complexity associated with full authoring packages.

www.derby.ac.uk/cedm/mtlu/total.html

Getting Help for Your Institution:

TLTSN: Teaching and Learning Technology Support Network, provides free support and advice to UK higher education institutions on integrating technology into teaching and learning. This can include open-days and staff development seminars at your institution on generic issues and systems (WWW, Multimedia, VESOL, etc). (For subject-based queries about software etc. use the CTI).

www.tltp.ac.uk/tltsn

I am Director of the Derby TLTSN Centre, and you can find information about this, as well as information about VESOL, VELAB, VideoNet, the Derby Learning Centre, plus hot links to useful sites of relevance to staff and educational development at:

www.derby.ac.uk/cedm/welcome.html